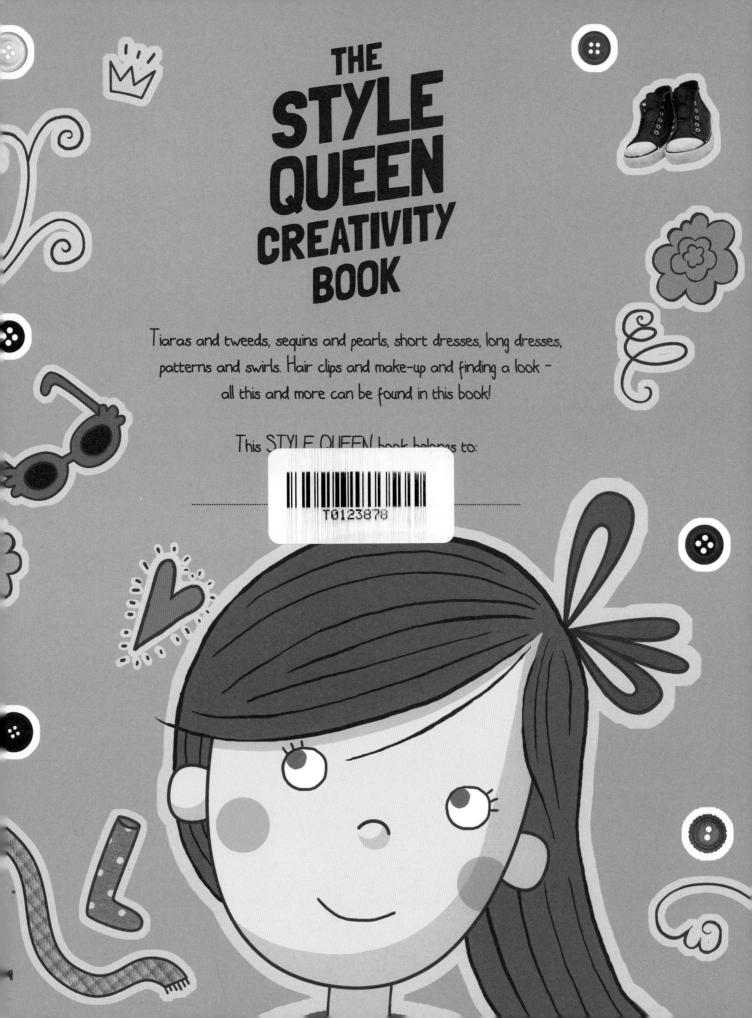

THE STYLE QUEEN CREATIVITY BOOK

Tiaras and tweeds, sequins and pearls, short dresses, long dresses, patterns and swirls. Hair clips and make-up and finding a look – all this and more can be found in this book!

This STYLE QUEEN book belongs to:

T0123878

What's inside this book?

Stories and pictures

There are plenty of places for super style queens to write, draw and paint in this book, so why not get going now!

Stickers

You will find your style queen stickers at the back of the book. Use them on the sticker scenes, quiz pages and anywhere else you want to!

Top puzzle fun...

...includes join the dots, a tricky maze, spot the differences, matching pairs and a testing style queen quiz!

Things to make

Make badges on page 25, fashion dolls on page 29, rose petal perfume on page 40, a necklace on page 53 and some slumber party invites on page 61. Look out for the fashion paper on page 12 as well!

Games

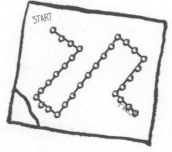

Who will reach the last outfit at the fancy dress shop on page 8 or be the best at the memory game on page 73? Will it be you?

This is a Carlton book
Text, design and illustration copyright
© Carlton Books Limited 2011, 2019

First published in 2011
by Carlton Books Limited
an imprint of the Carlton Publishing Group,
20 Mortimer Street, London, W1T 3JW
This edition published in 2019

10 9 8 7 6 5 4 3 2 1

ISBN: 978 1 78312 474 9

Printed and bound in China

Author: **Andrea Pinnington**
Consultant: **Sally Stiletto**
Design: **Zoë Dissell at Snowy Design**
Illustrations: **Smiljana Coh (with Fabio Leone) and Elle Ward**

This book was made by Andrea Pinnington for the style queen Ellie Nobelle.

Style queen invitation

Do you have what it takes to be a super style queen?

Hello, my name is Gemma and this is my dog, Sparkle. We would like to invite you on a magical journey into the glamorous world of fashion. Just complete the activities then claim your super STYLE QUEEN award.

IF YOU DO, THEN PLEASE TURN THE PAGE...

All about me...

This notebook is TOP SECRET! Intruders – no peeking!

My fashion name is...

•••••••••••••••••••••••••••••••••

This is ME!
Seriously stylish!

This was the number of candles on my last birthday cake.

I have (tick the right answers)...

☐ ...cute curly hair   ☐ ...silky, straight hair   ☐ ...scrummy short hair   ☐ ...lovely long hair

My favourite song is...

....

The outfits that make me look like a true style queen are...

....

My prettiest jewellery is...

....

I look good in (tick the right answers)...

☐   ☐   ☐

☐   ☐   ☐

How to draw a style queen

Copy each step-by-step drawing into the boxes below.

First, draw an oval for her head, then two shapes like these ones for her body.

Now, give her a neck, some little sleeves, then draw in the tops of her legs.

Good start!

Getting there!

Try drawing some more style queens on your doodle page (see page 70).

Next, give her a high pony tail, some arms, a belt and some stylish boots.

Finally, draw in her face, decorate her clothes and give her some accessories!

Almost done!

GREAT WORK!

Fancy-dress dash

You have been invited to a fancy-dress party but there's only one outfit left at the costume shop. Be the first to get there!

HOW TO PLAY:

You will need a die and something you can use for counters (like buttons).

1 Place your counters on START and take it in turns to roll the die – the first one to roll a 6 goes first.

2 MOVE FORWARD the number of squares shown on the die then follow the instructions written on the squares.

3 The first person to reach the fancy-dress shop is the WINNER.

START
1
2
3
4
5
6
7
8
9
10
11
12
13

A neighbour lends you his skateboard. Go forward 2.

Your shoe breaks. Stop to get it repaired. Miss a go.

Find yourself accidentally in a sweetie shop. Miss a go.

Find some magic sneakers that carry you to 16.

Take a short cut through an alley. Go on to 11.

Alley

One of your friends lends you a bike. Ride on to 13.

Stop to eat yummy cakes at Miss Hannah's Muffin Parlour. Miss a go.

Amazing things to do with your fashion paper

1. Cut out the CLOTHES on the back of your fashion paper. Use them to dress your fashion dolls (see page 29) and, hey presto, another style queen job well done!

2. Draw more outfits on the back of some wrapping paper. Cut them out and use them to create a shimmering FASHION COLLAGE.

3. Get a large piece of card, any leftover fashion paper and a pile of old magazines. Go through them all and cut out any outfits, patterns and colours that you like. Stick them onto the card and you will start to see your own FASHION STYLE develop.

4. Try designing some of your own FABRIC PATTERNS. Use the circles below to practise in.

Perfect patterns

Cut along the dotted lines shown here and on page 14, then turn to page 30 to find out what to do next.

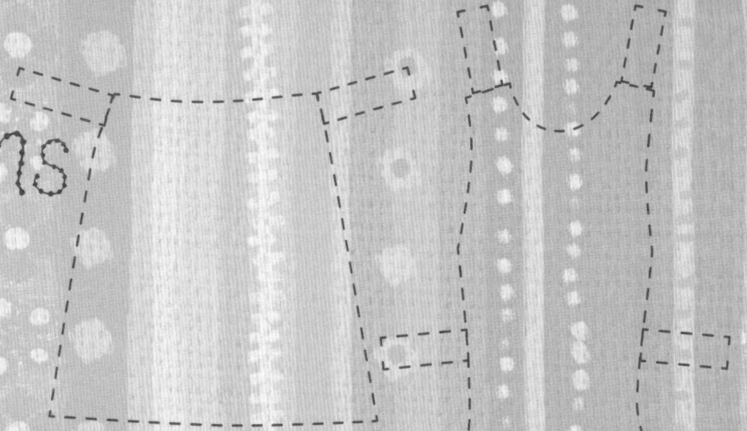

Mad as a hatter

Join the dots to reveal the latest hat sensation.

11
12
16
15
17
13
18
10
7
19
21
22
14
8
23
9
20
24
5
6
26
25
27
3
30
29
28
2
1
35
31
4
34
32
33

Answer is at the back of the book.

Choose some clothes from below and draw them on the fairy opposite.

hats

tops

skirts

wands

shoes

Fairy fashions

This little fashion fairy just can't decide what to wear today. Perhaps you can help her...

little hat →

gossamer top →

← sparkly wand

← shimmery skirt

Give a name to your fairy

soft, silky shoes

Pretty things

Colour in this beautiful jewellery.

All in a day's work

Complete the outfits of these two busy people.

cute
ponytail

impressive
shoes

FLIGHT ATTENDANT

TENNIS CHAMPION

Spot the difference

Can you spot **10** differences between these hairdressing pictures?

Answers are at the back of the book.

Fabulous faces

Draw some lovely make-up on these girls.

dazzling

sophisticated

natural

brightly coloured

scary

Model muddle

Unhappy about being the latest fashion accessories, these pets have tangled up their leads.

Foofoo

Coco

Meringue

Stella

Crumble

Jasper

Which pet belongs to which model?

Answers are at the back of the book..

How to make a badge

Turn the page to find out what to do next.

Style Queen

Birthday Girl

1 CUT OUT the badge you want to wear.

2 STICK it onto some card, then cut out the card shape.

3 TAPE a safety pin to the back of the badge.

4 ATTACH your badge to your clothes and see who notices it.

☆26☆

Fashion makeover

You are Phoebe Fortesque - top fashion designer!

Give these desperate dressers a new look.

Bunny

Bunny's friends have persuaded her to have a major makeover.

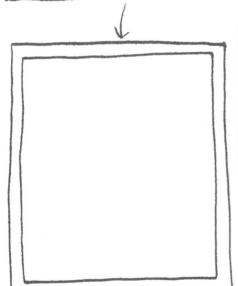

Wow, Phoebe, you've really given Bunny a new look. Amazing!

Darren

Darren doesn't like going out because people laugh at him. Phoebe, please help!

What a difference clothes can make! The new Darren is super confident!

Esme

Esme's dress sense is slightly unusual. Any ideas what to do, Phoebe?

No longer stuck on another planet, Esme's clothes are now really cool.

Where, oh where, is my lovely handbag?

START ↓

Silly Milly has left her favourite handbag on a bench where she was chatting.

Can you help Milly find her way back to the bench?

FINISH

Answer is at the back of the book.

Fabulous
fashion dolls

Turn the page to find out what to do with your dolls.

What to do with your fashion dolls:

1 Ask a grown-up to help you CUT this page out of the book.

2 STICK the dolls onto a stiff piece of card, then get a grown-up to help you to cut out each doll shape.

3 Next, CUT out the clothes shapes on the back of your fashion paper (see pages 11 and 14).

4 WRAP the clothes you want to use around the dolls. Use the paper tabs to hold them in position.

5 MAKE your own card doll shapes and extra clothes. You could try making animal shapes and costumes as well.

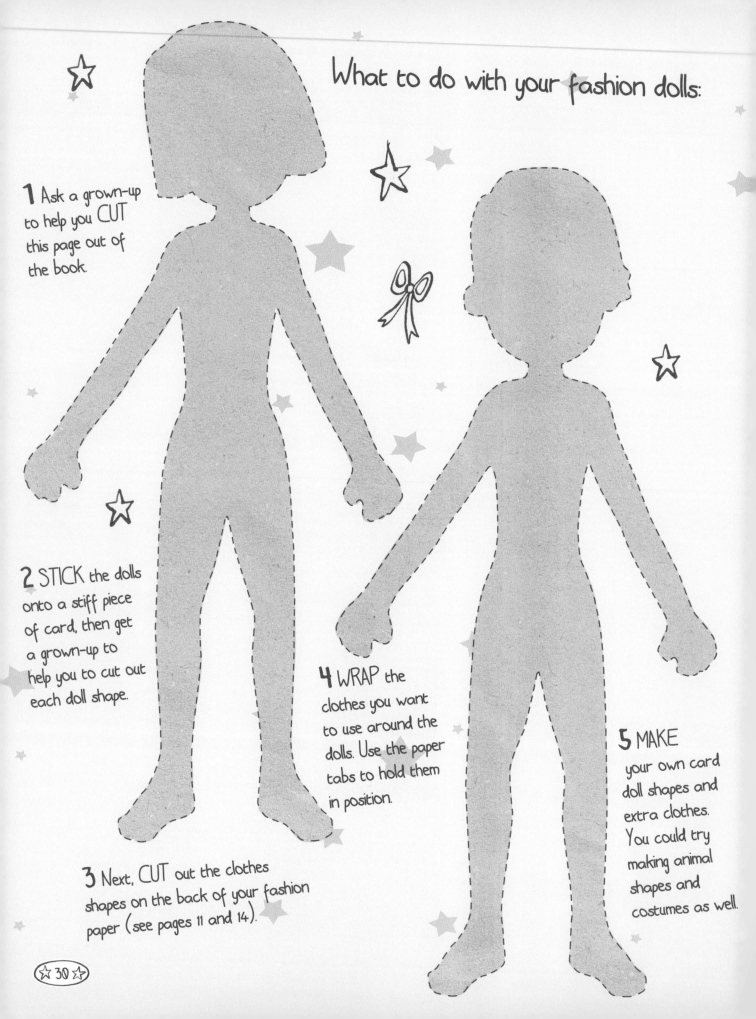

one of a kind

Do you want to stand out in the crowd?
Decorate these items to make them truly unique.

hearts?

What would you wear?

...at a beach party?

...if you were a pop star?

Lots of space for using your stylish stickers and coloured pencils.

...at a fun fair?

...at a slumber party?

Ready to wear

Design an outfit for every season of the year.

Spring sensation

Summer sizzler

Autumn arrival

Winter wonder

Me time!

Fill the shelves and dressing table with your favourite beauty things.

jewellery stand

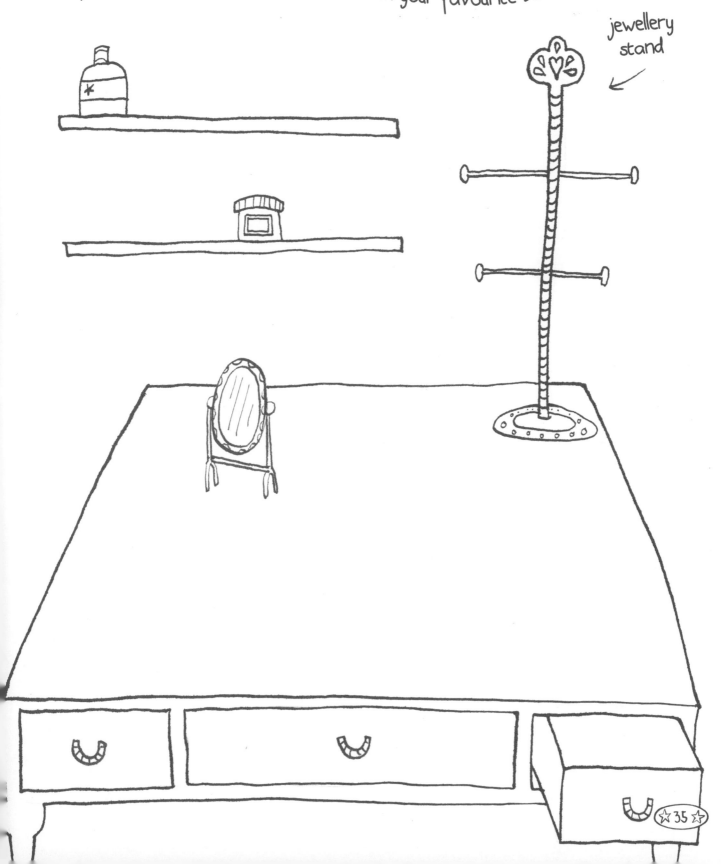

My little fashion diary

It's fun to keep a record of what you wear!

MONDAY

— — — — — — — — — — — —

— — — — — — — — — — — —

TOP TIP: Wear something really bright today.

Draw some pictures, too.

TUESDAY

_____

_____

_____

TOP TIP: It's accessories day! Go wild making things match.

WEDNESDAY

— — — — — — — — — — — —

— — — — — — — — — — — —

TOP TIP: Try a new hairstyle – bunchies, pony tail or a zig-zag parting?

THURSDAY

TOP TIP: Smell beautiful today!

FRIDAY

TOP TIP: Borrow an outfit from a friend.

SATURDAY

TOP TIP: A bit of girly pampering goes a long way - relax in a bubble bath.

SUNDAY

TOP TIP: Spring clean! Get rid of clothes you've grown out of.

Decorate a shoe ☆

Colour in some daring designs on these fabulous shoes.

How to make ROSE-PETAL perfume

When you've nothing else to do and you're bored of watching telly, here's the perfect thing to make – something pink and sweet and smelly.

You will need:
2 handfuls of rose petals
2 cups of water

What you need to do:

1 Find a bottle to store your perfume in (decorate it if you want to).

2 Measure 2 cups of water and pour them into a pan.

3 Place a lid on the pan and bring the water to a slow boil (ask a grown-up to help you).

4 Turn off the heat and add the rose petals. Leave the mixture until cool.

5 Strain the mixture and squeeze the petals.

6 Fill the bottle and use your new ROSE-PETAL PERFUME!

Name that scent

Think of some names for the perfume in these pretty bottles.

Bubblicious

Pampered pet

Copy this sausage dog into the empty frame below. Try drawing one square at a time.

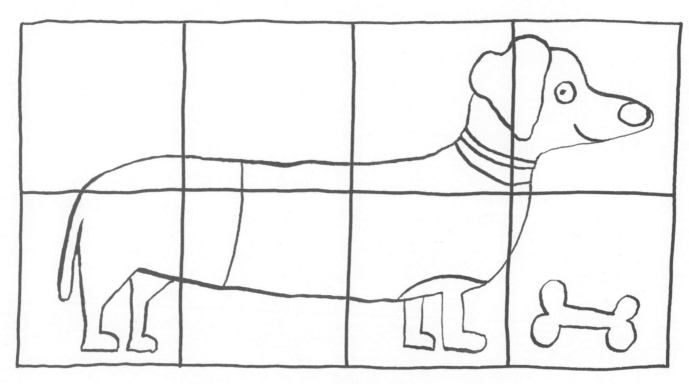

Give him a lovely patterned coat as well.

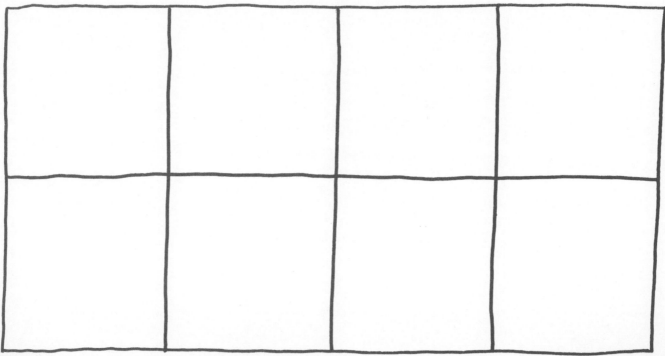

Call me!

Design a fabulous new range
of retro mobile-phone cases.

Leave some text
messages
on them, too.

How to paint your nails

The perfect way to get great results!

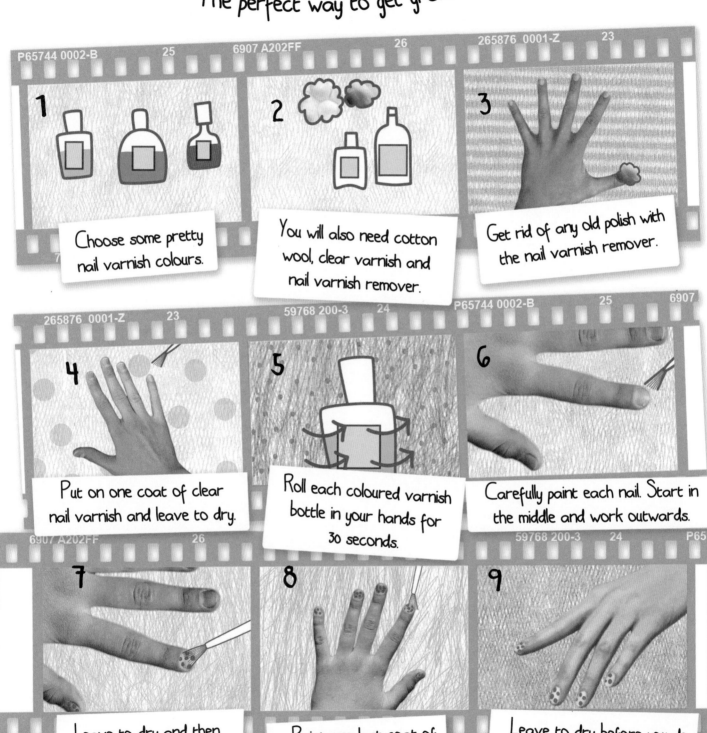

1 Choose some pretty nail varnish colours.

2 You will also need cotton wool, clear varnish and nail varnish remover.

3 Get rid of any old polish with the nail varnish remover.

4 Put on one coat of clear nail varnish and leave to dry.

5 Roll each coloured varnish bottle in your hands for 30 seconds.

6 Carefully paint each nail. Start in the middle and work outwards.

7 Leave to dry and then add other colours if you want to.

8 Paint one last coat of clear varnish.

9 Leave to dry before you do anything with your hands.

Be a nail artist

Make up your own amazing nail designs and draw them in below.
Then try them out on your own nails.

red with
white
spots

glittery
tips

pink and
purple
diagonal
stripes

Design workshop

Draw some gorgeous patterns
on this year's hot swimwear.

splodge

flower power

animal print

hearts and stars

wild thing

spotty dotty

plain and simple

fancy

How to hold a fashion show

Get your friends to dress up in their favourite outfits and practise being fashion models.

1 Ask a grown-up to help you CUT this page out of the book along the dotted line.

2 Turn over the page and FILL IN the details about where and when the show will be (for example: "My bedroom, 5:30, Tuesday").

3 COLOUR IN the dress on the model.

4 PUT UP the poster in a place where your friends will see it.

5 The day before the show, SORT OUT your clothes and work out what you are going to model. Ask your friends to do the same.

6 On the day, prepare some tasty snacks and drinks to serve during the show. Get dressed into your outfit, turn on the music and LET THE SHOW BEGIN!

You are invited to a FASHION SHOW

Date:

Time:

Place:

Outfits on show:

Why not colour in this dress?

The emperor's new clothes

This is a well-known tale about an emperor who makes a fool of himself. Pretend you are a famous writer and tell the story in your own words. You don't need to know it, you can just make up anything you like!

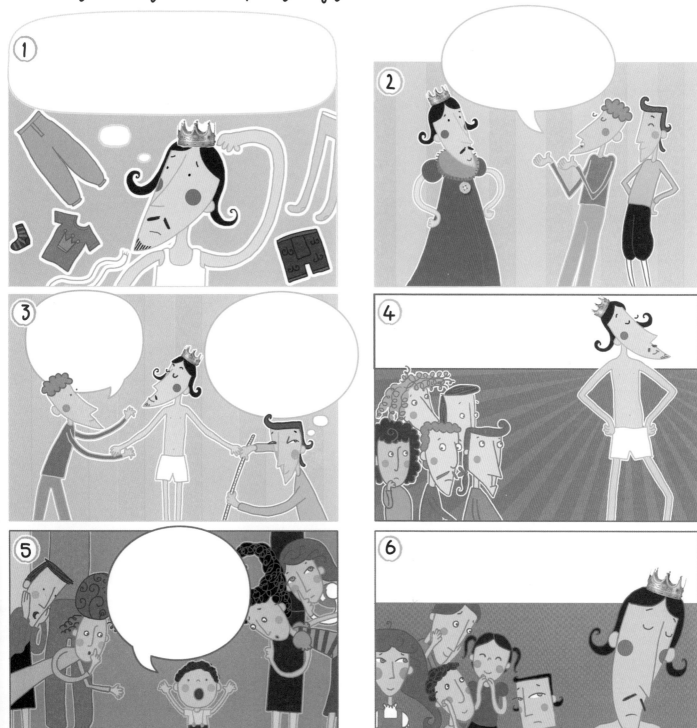

Down at the salon...

Why not try something different with your hair?
(Ask a grown-up to help you if you get stuck.)

How to plait your hair

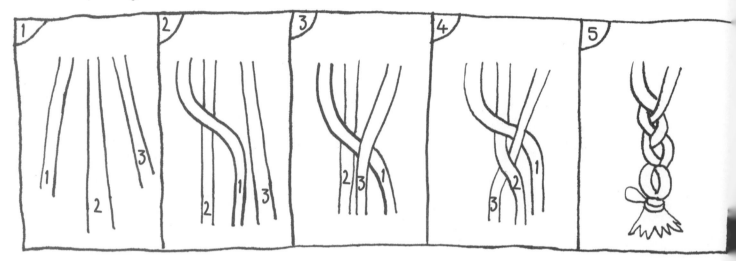

1	2	3	4	5
Divide your hair into 3 strands.	Put the first strand over the second.	Then, put the third strand over the first	Next, put the second strand over the third.	Repeat these steps to the end, then secure with a tie.

How to make a zig-zag parting

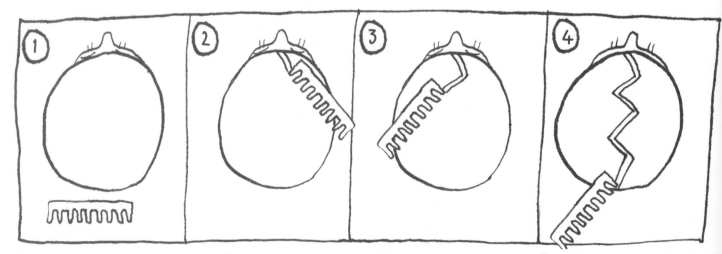

1	2	3	4
Brush your hair until it is silky smooth.	Take a comb and part your hair like this.	Then, part the next section going the opposite way.	Zig-zag your parting like this until you reach the back of your head.

That really suits you!

Draw a hairstyle for each of these characters.

princess

baby

actress

wizard

teenager

school boy

bride

goblin

TOP GIRL

Draw yourself onto the front cover of this magazine's summer edition.

How to make a paper-bead necklace

Finished paper-bead necklace

You will need:
- old magazines or paper and pens
- a length of string or strong thread
- scissors (always ask a grown-up to help you use them)
- glue

What to do:

1 TEAR out some colourful magazine pages or draw some patterns onto a piece of paper.

2 CUT the paper into long triangles and put a dab of glue at the small ends.

3 ROLL each triangle towards the small end leaving a hole in the middle. Then roll it round a pencil, which you remove once the bead is made. Stick the ends together.

4 REPEAT this with lots of triangles until you have enough paper beads to make a necklace.

5 MEASURE and CUT a length of thread or string long enough to make a necklace or bracelet.

6 THREAD your beads on and tie securely or fit a clasp to the ends if you have one.

Mirror, mirror on the wall

Take a look in a real mirror...

...then draw your reflection in this one.

Fashion disasters!

What are these funkily dressed people saying?

Matching pairs

Draw a line between the socks and gloves that go together.

Answers are at the back of the book.

seeing double

Can you spot the 3 differences between each set of twins?

1 ....

2 ....

3 ....

Serena and Sasha

Poppy and Peaches

1 ....

2 ....

3 ....

Orlando and Archibald

1 ....

2 ....

3 ....

Answers are at the back of the book.

A day at the races

Draw some magnificent hats onto the racegoers below, then colour in their outfits.

Where in the world?

Colour in these costumes from around the world. You can use the colours shown at the bottom of the page or make up some of your own.

Spain

Holland

Peru

China

India

Africa

Slumber party

Cut out these invitations and send them to your friends.

_____

is invited to a
Slumber party!

on: _____

at: _____

_____

is invited to a
sleepover!

on: _____

at: _____

Don't forget to bring your...
- ☐ nightwear
- ☐ slippers
- ☐ toothbrush
- ☐ teddy
- ☐ midnight feast*

   *ask a grown-up first!

Don't forget to bring your...
- ☐ nightwear
- ☐ slippers
- ☐ toothbrush
- ☐ teddy
- ☐ midnight feast*

   *ask a grown-up first!

Amazing things to do with your stickers

1 See if you can find the right stickers to go on the style queen pages that follow. You can also play with them over and over again on the fold out STICKER SCENES at the end of the book.

2 Look out for these other pages where you can use your STICKERS:
What would you wear? - page 32
Ready to wear - page 34
Me time! - page 35
My little fashion diary - page 36
On the catwalk - page 67
Movie premiere! - page 76

3 Fashion designers are always collecting useful bits and pieces to use in future projects. Use the stickers to decorate empty JAM JARS and then store buttons, clips, bows, ribbons and other useful objects in them.

4 Create your own FASHION LABEL. Think up a name for the sort of clothes you would like to design, then create your own fashion label stationery using the stickers for decoration. You could make notelets, invitations to fashion events, cards and letters, all with your own fashion label name on them.

Find the missing stickers

Answers are at the back of the book.

Something to make
you smell beautiful.

Every girl should
have one.

Super
sticker
quiz

Which stickers belong
in these circles?

Emergency repair kit
for style queens.

You might need a pair
of these in winter.

You don't want
to lose these.

Answers are at the back of the book.

Born to ✳✳✳✳✳?

Join the dots to find out what this girl is doing.

18
19
20
17
21
16
22
15
23
28 29
12 13 14 24 25 31
7 34 30 32
27
11
26
8
35 33
6
36
5 4 37
3 42
2 38
43
41
39
40
1
44

Answer is at the back of the book.

On the catwalk

Read the descriptions, then draw the models into the spotlights below.

Persephone looks fabulous in this magenta mini-skirt with contrasting tangerine top. Set to be one of this season's MUST HAVES.

January is UTTERLY GORGEOUS in this apricot bikini with matching picnic basket. The use of foil is striking.

Pomegranate's flaming red hair sets off this velvet romper suit perfectly. The pink wellies are an AWESOME addition.

Are those pyjamas or day wear? Who cares! The pretty flowers look so delicate against Zoë's pale skin. WOW!

What sort of style queen are you?

Complete the quiz, then find out what your score means. Circle your answers.

Which SHOE do you like the most?

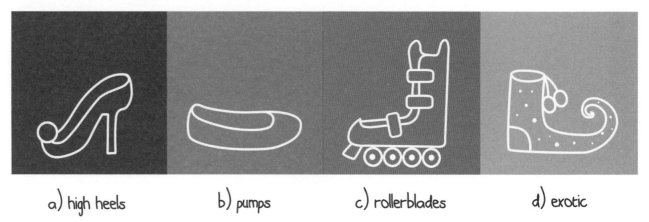

a) high heels   b) pumps   c) rollerblades   d) exotic

How do you like to wear your HAIR?

a) glamorous   b) natural   c) practical   d) unusual

Do you prefer...

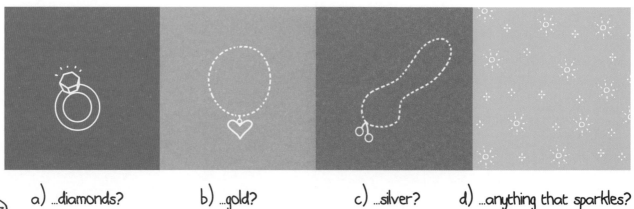

a) ...diamonds?   b) ...gold?   c) ...silver?   d) ...anything that sparkles?

What sort of CLOTHES do you like wearing most of all?

a) smart clothes   b) anything you can find   c) sporty clothes   d) interesting and unusual clothes

HOW DID YOU SCORE?

Mostly A

You certainly know how to dress up for a party! Your smart clothes and careful dressing will get you noticed. You'll go far!

Mostly B

You don't need to spend much time on how you look – your natural beauty and charm will get you through life. Way to go!

Mostly C

You are an outdoor kind of girl. You need the right kit for your activities but dressing up is so not your thing. Impressive!

Mostly D

You don't follow fashion trends, you make them! Your interesting clothes makes us think that you could be a future fashion designer. You are definitely one to watch!

Mix of all 4: You are a constant surprise and like to keep people guessing!

Fashion doodles...

Pretend to be a top fashion designer and create some lovely designs on this special drawing paper.

Keeping cool

Draw some pretty patterns on these fans, then colour them in.

How to make a fabulous fan

Draw a pattern on one side of some paper, then fold it back and forth.

Open the paper out and glue a lolly stick to each end.

Refold it and fasten the end of the sticks together.

Just imagine...

Write some funny words in these speech bubbles.

What is this serious shopper thinking?

What are these two girls fighting about?

What's inside my handbag?

Look at these objects for a minute, then turn the page and draw all the things you can remember.

hairband

pen

hairbrush

sunglasses

sunscreen

lip balm

purse

My little fashion diary

music player

lollipop

What can you remember?

Draw in all the things that were in the handbag on the previous page.

NO PEEKING!

A long time ago...
...this dress was the latest fashion!

Draw in the other half of this lady.

Movie premiere!

Use your stickers and colouring pencils here.

5 good reasons why I'm a style queen

1. I always
....

2. I hate
....

3. I love to
....

4. I wear
....

5. I have never
....

signed by
....

Fashion award

presented to

· ·

for being a

SENSATIONAL
STYLE QUEEN

signed by

· ·

for The House of Fashion

15

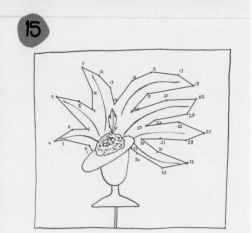

20

23

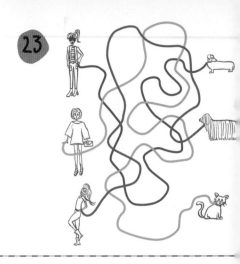

The
STYLE QUEEN
Creativity Book Answers

♡

28

56

57 Seeing Double

Serena and Sasha
1 Hair
2 Collar
3 Hair clip

Poppy and Peache
1 Hair
2 Earrings
3 Bracelet

Orlando and Archibald
1 Freckles
2 Elbow pads
3 Hair

64

65

66